ALSO BY KEVIN YOUNG

POETRY
Blue Laws: Selected & Uncollected Poems 1995–2015
Book of Hours
Ardency
Dear Darkness
For the Confederate Dead
To Repel Ghosts: The Remix
Black Maria
Jelly Roll: A Blues
To Repel Ghosts
Most Way Home

NONFICTION
Bunk: The Rise of Hoaxes, Humbug, Plagiarists, Phonies,
Post-Facts, and Fake News
The Grey Album: On the Blackness of Blackness

AS EDITOR
The Hungry Ear: Poems of Food & Drink
The Collected Poems of Lucille Clifton 1965–2010 (with Michael S. Glaser)
Best American Poetry 2011
The Art of Losing: Poems of Grief & Healing
Jazz Poems
John Berryman: Selected Poems
Blues Poems
Giant Steps: The New Generation of African American Writers

BROWN

BROWN

POEMS

Kevin Young

· Photographs by Melanie Dunea ·

 ALFRED A. KNOPF | NEW YORK | 2020

THIS IS A BORZOI BOOK
PUBLISHED BY ALFRED A. KNOPF

Copyright © 2018 by Kevin Young
Photographs © 2018 Melanie Dunea
All rights reserved.
Published in the United States by Alfred A. Knopf,
a division of Penguin Random House LLC, New York,
and distributed in Canada by Random House of Canada, a division of
Penguin Random House Canada Limited, Toronto.
www.aaknopf.com/poetry
Knopf, Borzoi Books, and the colophon
are registered trademarks of Penguin Random House LLC.

Library of Congress Cataloging-in-Publication Data
Names: Young, Kevin, [date] author.
Title: Brown : poems / Kevin Young.
Description: First edition. | New York : Alfred A. Knopf, 2018.
Identifiers: LCCN 2017029270 (print) | LCCN 2017030884 (ebook) |
ISBN 9781524732554 (ebook) | ISBN 9781524732547 (hardcover) |
ISBN 9781524711146 (trade pbk.)
Subjects: LCSH: African Americans—Poetry | BISAC: POETRY / American /
African American. | POETRY / American / General.
Classification: LCC PS3575.O798 (ebook) | LCC PS3575.O798 A6 2018 (print) |
DDC 811/.54—dc23
LC record available at https://lccn.loc.gov/2017029270

Cover illustration by Jason Kernevich
Cover design by Kelly Blair
Endpapers by Mack Young

Manufactured in the United States of America
Published April 18, 2018
First Paperback Edition, March 5, 2020

CONTENTS

FIELD RECORDINGS

THREE · NIGHT TRAIN

FOUR · THE CRESCENT LIMITED

BROWN

Thataway

And the migrants kept coming.
—JACOB LAWRENCE

Was walking. Was
walking & then waiting
for a train, the 12:40
to take us thataway.
(I got there early.)
Wasn't a train
exactly but a chariot
or the Crescent Limited come
to carry me some
home I didn't yet
know. There were those
of us not ready till good
Jim swung from a tree
& the white folks crowded
the souvenir photo's frame—
let his body black-
en, the extremities
shorn—not shed,
but skimmed off
so close it can be shaving
almost. An ear
in a pocket, on a shelf,
a warning where a book
could go. So
I got there early.
See now, it was morning—
a cold snap, first frost
which comes even
here & kills the worms
out the deer. You can
hunt him then
but we never did want,
after, no trophy
crowned down
from a wall, watching—
just a meal, what
we might make last

3

till spring. There are ways
of keeping a thing.
Then there are ways
of leaving, & also
the one way. That
we didn't want.
I got there early.
Luggage less sturdy
(cardboard, striped, black)
than my hat. Shoebox
of what I shan't say
lunch on my lap.
The noise the rails made
even before the train.
A giant stomach growling.
A bowed belly. I did
not pray. I got there
early. It was not
no wish, but a way.

HOME RECORDINGS

"Of course I cannot understand it," he said. "If your heads were stuffed with straw, like mine, you would probably all live in the beautiful places, and then Kansas would have no people at all. It is fortunate for Kansas that you have brains."

—THE SCARECROW
The Wizard of Oz

ONE

The A Train

Swing

If, up early,
    an hour no jazzster
never did see,

    my son & I—
he's three—
    jump up to accompany

Mister Charlie
    Christian on his six string,
listening to *Swing*

    to Bop (Live), a recording cut
long after midnight—
    my son plucky

on the tiny tourist
    toy guitar his big sis
brought back from Fiji,

    tapping his feet
while I rake
    the plastic strings

of my ancient, resurrected
    racquetball racquet
that showed up lately—

    strumming the sun,
the morning
    into being—my son

stopping to chase the dust
    we can suddenly see
in the bright now falling—

    his skinny legs
jangling—you'll
    maybe understand,

later, when he runs in
    & asks,
Daddy,

    what's jazz?
I just point at him
    & laugh.

Rumble in the Jungle

If you didn't know
    better, you might think
Muhammad was praying,

not talking smack—
    arms up, Ali
leans way back

as if trying to catch
    a glimpse
of the Almighty—

he's told no one
    his plan
to rope-a-dope—

to bend in whatever wind
    Foreman sends
or knocks out of him.

Haymakers & body
    blows. The thumbs
of his old-fashioned boxing gloves

upright like Ali
    hopes to hitch a ride
to heaven. Instead he's here

in Zaire, stuck waiting
    for the monsoon—
playing possum

through seven rounds
    till it's time to climb & jab
his way off the ropes

like Tarzan sawing free
    from a fishing net in a Saturday
matinee—swinging

till Foreman backstrokes
    to the floor. Seven whole rounds
of reckoning—till a woman

in a dashiki, stepping lightly,
    carries the card
for the next round filled

with what now
    appears omen, inevitability—
for one moment

the number 8
    knocked flat
on its side—

an infinity.

Open Letter to Hank Aaron

Your folded jersey said it
    best: *Brave*. A bounty
on your head, last name a prophet's,

    first a king, you kept swinging
that hammer, Bad Henry, even after
    the threats fell like hail.

Every barbershop's expert
    already knew you would best
Ruth's sacred record, just

    like they knew the Babe
was really black, ever
    see that nose of his?

The hate mail you quit opening
    kept coming, scrawled or sutured,
brushing you back more

    than a Hoot Gibson inside pitch,
no return address—
    the newspaper with your obit

already written, primed
    to run. Still you swung
like a boxer in the late rounds

    hoping to change the Judges'
minds—once you connect
    & the ball barely sails

over the short porch in left,
    you don't so much run
as pace

    around the bases—
nonchalant, nervous—a man
    with too much cash

worrying his pockets, a windfall
   he may never live
long enough to spend.

   Rounding second,
two guys race
   up to you, friend

or foe, clapping you
   on the back—
I hear they're doctors now—

   as if you'd just been born.
Hopping the fence
   like that ball did,

your mama
   bear-hugs you
headed home. *Think of it*

   as money,
the Bancard billboard
   you cleared in left

field says. Not
   that you did—
after, the microphones

   aimed at your face
like arrows into a saint,
   your face less belief

than relief—
   I just thank God,
you say, *it's over with.*

   Falling back
into the crowd, unharmed,
   you wave your blue arms.

now thrown around us—
    in dusk
our boys' bodies grow

    as hard to see
as hope.
    I think of how

when first invented,
    the flying
disc was free

    & what cost—
tonight you can
    almost feel it—

was the invisible rope.

Phys. Ed.

[WARM UP]

Between Language & Health
    perched Gym or Phys. Ed.
or whatever they called our removing

what fit & changing into our clashing
    school colors. My t-shirt dubbed me
YOUNG, something barkable, one

syllable. Those without uniforms
    lost grades or got loans; those
with boners in the showers

got beat up. Edsel, once caught
    beating off in a stall, would rub
the backs of his knees with green

deodorant, he said to keep cool—
    this, long before we heard how to stop
sweating & smell, lectured in the male art

of antiperspirant while the seventh-grade
    girls learned about blood
during third period. That talk

we only got wind of later.

[TUMBLING]

Stringer was a rumor,
    former Olympic wrestler
now overweight gym teacher

sent down river
    to Marjorie French Middle School
for hurtling some poor fool

who told him off in high school
    down the stairs. A whole
bloody flight. Once

his ham-sized elbow staked my chest
    to demonstrate pain—
a pin—his face a fist.

Floundered high & dry,
    glasses-less, I counted rafters
blurry & regular

as the times Stringer yanked out
    the tucked shirts of handstood girls
whenever he spotted their legs,

laughing. How often he stared
    while they changed—
those girls who tumbled

while we wrestled—
    Stringer playing
pocket-pool

& losing, scratching
    himself, all eightball,
no cue.

[DODGEBALL]

When Mrs. Ostrich blew
   the whistle, the whole
high school knew

that meant business—she'd call
   us sissies
or girls for running

too slow. Lazy himself, after
   teaching Study Hall, Coach Gray
had a cow if we looked at all

tired but put in a soft word,
   a *good hustle* for every
Amy or awkward devil

who couldn't swing
   to save their lives, much less
break a tie. He never

bothered to teach them
   a thing. The gym echoed
the tons of times those two

coaches met, hidden among
   the Driver's Ed cars
or the dull

steel-tipped arrows
   & half-deflated dodgeballs
that hibernate till spring—

the duo doing
   their tug-oh-
war thing.

[BLEACHERS]

Johnny Henry, no angel, managed
    to wrestle one—not the father
who beat him silly, not his mother

who'd split or the seventh grade that could
    smell him coming; nor the health teacher
who taught Johnny how to wash & not go

in his pants; nor Coach De Mann who gave him sneakers
    for gym, making him wait so everyone knew
the poor white kid was him—but one short

school year later, his chest grown half as wide
    as his height, Johnny Henry could lift
more than twice his weight

off the bench press, smear
    other kids with some newfound
strength. What could anyone say then,

pinned like a butterfly to the mat? He won
    every meet we wrestled, met
each opponent like a seraphim,

many limbed, wiping
    the smiles from chubby
cherubs, putting them in a cradle

or ball & chain while we stomped
    the stands, chanting
Pin! Pin!—the bleachers

calling again
    again his brave
two-fisted name.

[PRACTICE]

Each afternoon for hours
    our bodies weren't
our own—we'd have

to run, give Coach
    twenty,
then *Ready: Wrassle.*

Nabus, nicknamed
    Tonka cause he was squat
& tough as those toy trucks,

could climb the gym's ropes
    thirty feet using only
his hands. Once

I watched him
    about to be pinned, then
stand up with a kid

across his hairless chest
    & slam him for the win.
With some whale splayed

on our stomachs,
    we'd practice bridges
arcing on our heads

for hours, hoping to build
    necks & break
chokeholds like backs.

I still have the letter
    jacket, won mostly
by making 98 weight

all fall easy.
    Still I'd drink
only spit

for days, swallowing
   insults about my family
& skin, the way

teammates would call you *spook*
   then beg you for food
before a meet. On buses

boys practiced becoming adults—
   lying about girls,
playing rock, paper,

scissors for pain—then rubbing
   the ears of enemies
till they bloomed

into cauliflowers. Whenever
   anyone asked
to share, I'd hock

into my sandwiches,
   put the halves back
together, then swallow

them slow.

[CITY]

In his office, Coach De Mann said
   I had it made & could win
City if only I put my mind

where my body was, applied
   myself. That season I lifted,
ran stairs, wore three layers

of sweats to slim sleep. All winter
   in trash bags I jogged to Russia & back,
dreamt steak, no fat. The drinking

fountain we ran laps past
   ringed in launched loogies
stayed unsipped.

On the meet-bound bus
   I watched boys spit out pounds
in Kwik cups—heard tell

of magic saunas & miracle,
   ten-pound
dumps. One Coach made my friend

drop a whole class, cutting
   from 112 to 105 overnight;
Tim bought PMS pills to lose

water, the cashier staring back
   at him blank as his Biology
test the next day

when he passed out cold. Watched
   another kid shave—rusty razor,
no cream, no mirror—

when some ref deemed
   his teenage stubble
a weapon—

in the warped
   metal of the paper towel dispenser
his chin bloomed stigmata.

After I told Mom I knew I'd win
   she only half-
believed me, said hope

was good to have. Later I waved
   to her from the podium
after winning City, my smile as long

as the shot she'd thought I had.
   How I loved
Coach & his belief,

the medal mine. Earning
   my letter jacket's giant T,
I was called to his office, I thought

to shake hands. Instead he asked,
   You can dance, right?
Why don't I moonwalk

for him & the boys?
   A ring of fellow coaches grinned.
Stunned, I did not laugh

or dance or do that backwards
   glide he wanted—I still haven't a clue
which race he thought

he'd have me run—my medal
   long lost—that sunny morning
right before Life

Science, long after History.

Ice Storm, 1984

The lines for power & speech
     freeze, then stiffen & fall—
thrown back into dark

we hear the radio tell the town
     what we already know—
last night's storm iced over

everything, yet hurt only
     half Topeka's houses—wiping
away windows, we see some

homes, doors down, still bright
     & inviting as snow. Here our heat
has ended—we have only wood

& whatever warmth
     won't escape
like gossip. Power out,

our freezer starts to thaw—
     we keep meat out back in drifts.
USD 501, name like a grade

of beef, cancels—
     no Civics, no Language
class, no Western Civilization.

How many mornings
     had I stalled, dressing
by the faint radio, praying

the airwaves would list
     my school among the saved?
By evening, the thrill of hooky sours

as our house pours
     into dark & cold, nothing
like the brief candle-warmth

of brownouts when lightning
          would keep us from touching
metal, or each other, for fear

of shock. Dusk starts
          here like horror-movie
houses abandoned

& adrift—phone line
          cut like an anchor,
the killer in shadow

behind every door. Nothing
          lasts—neither food
nor warmth, yet Dad

won't leave our glacial living
          room, stubborn
as the mule we'd ride around

unsaddled down home. He burns
          wood while Mom gathers
our things & her son, saying

she's had enough dark
          childhood nights to outlast
a life. Heading blocks

away it feels we cross
          a century—tiptoe
through the blackout

across slick, lit ice
          to our neighbors' kind house
full of bright bulbs, running

water. We've arrived.
          Civilization, Mom laughs.
In their carpeted

basement rec room, I shoot
      pinball when the son
lets me play—the coffin talks

if hit with
      enough English—
after he flips off the lights

our faces flicker in the pretend night
      like the father I picture
by the hearth, fire dying

like laughter. Who knows what
      he eats, curled up
mammoth & woolen

with a fifth aged
      amber as skin.
Phoneless, we return days later

to find him, unmoved,
      shivering, in a quilt
his mother saved scraps for

& sewed. Beside him
      the bottle of blended empty
as a promise, as this house

half paid for. An hour later
      power returns—bless the company
electric—our heater starting up

its argument with the fridge.
      Will take far longer
till the stomach

in the freezer fills up & quits
      growling, for men to resurrect
the phone lines, our talk

trapped outside in ice.

History

Pillar of my high school, Mr. W
    made class by seven a.m., filling
his blackboards with white, using notes

    decades old & denture yellow.
I heard he could write any way
    you wanted—backward, forward,

left hand or right, even
    mirrored. For him History
was what each night

    he erased.
He never missed a day. Snow
    days drove the man insane—

    ———

regular as mail, he said if a letter could reach
    the school, so could we, trudging
through bitterest cold to his overwarm room.

    Never let kids eat, or talk in class, or take
down just what he wrote on the board—
    Listen to what I'm telling you, he'd say,

synthesize, don't record. Some days he'd launch
    into an anecdote about the War or
what's wrong with kids today—

you're not moral or immoral, just
    amoral. Even his jokes grown older
than he was, the trap door he wished he owned

    ———

    would send kids crashing into spikes
simply for walking during class
    without a pass. At breaks he began to bend

to pick up stray trash. He despised the *boom*
   boom boom of the radios black kids wore,
he swore, or tugged his eyes at the corners

   to imitate a Chinaman on the rail.
Ah, so. Brilliant is what everyone
   dubbed him, but by the time we got there

Mr. W had started to slip,
   missing most of the May before—
rumors went round

      ———

   our school had tried stopping
his return—*Take the year off,*
   you earned it—even he

told us that—but here he was,
   stonewalling, aged twenty years
over the summer, back like MacArthur

   or the Terminator to teach us
all. Some seniors from last year's class
   brought him steel tension balls

   that September—tinny things
he clutched in his palm & clanked past
   each other like cymbals

      ———

tolling stress. We
   stayed silent. Fifty pounds
shed over the summer, his wrists jutted out

   from the frayed cuffs
of his Crayola cardigans.
   He'd turn & tune

those chiming spheres like the globe
   his classroom never had—
his walls held only Old Glory

& a fading photo of the flag
raised at Iwo Jima. Mr. W let us know
    he never got to fight in the War

———

more often as the year wore
    away with his sweater's elbows,
till his yellow shirt shone

    through like yolk. That year
the Depression & World
    War took all winter

& knowing time was short, his own,
    Mr. W spent nights transcribing
to transparencies words

    water could wipe away,
numbering each palimpsest to match
    his crumbling notes. *Just in case,*

———

he'd say, above the overhead
    projector's buzz—*you could manage
without me.* He never

    could forget a past
only we would remember—
    his teacher telling him at graduation

*You know you're only seventeen
    & who knows how long this Pacific
Theater might last—They have this new*

    GI Bill. Get some college first,
Wayne, his name all alliteration,
    a tone poem. How

———

could he know
    we'd drop the bomb
& end it all? He tried serving

later, even went
to enlist in Korea but was foiled
    by a bad back & luck. *I tried,*

he'd plead the air. How to soothe
    a man who woke his whole life
at five & could silence kids

    not his own? Who once
drove 45 on the highway he told us
    cause Nixon asked

            ———

his fellow Americans to, counting
    each unpatriotic car that passed him
along the way? Like history he saved

    & scored the immeasurable—
with years-worth of sick days
    hoarded & never spent, illness

came to fetch him
    from the only other home he knew.
Wearing black now, pointing out

where other kids once sat long before
    we were born—future
governors, a crook or two—

            ———

    each chair a ghost. *You're my kids,*
he'd tell us, we built or broke
    his heart. Next day

he was gone. We never did make it
    to Vietnam—rest
of the year in silence we took down

    the words he'd written
projected on the wall
    like any man's promises to himself.

The latter half of the twentieth century
    felt a bit too cold, winter
lingered too long—Mr. W's words,

——

    unchanged, awaited
us *coloreds* & *women libbers*
    half-hoping for him

to return—for the world not to be
    as cruel as we'd learned.
We spent the Sixties

    minus Malcolm X, or Watts,
barely a March on Washington—
    all April & much

of May we waited for Woodstock
    & answers & assassinations
that would never come

——

    among the steady hum
& faint bright
    of flickering fluorescent lights.

Dictation

for William O'Neil,
FBI Informant

Teach yourself to swim. Borrowing a car
for a day, joyride eight leagues across
state lines. Catch yourself the moment

before the pigs catch you, hands white
on the wheel. You have the right to remain
etcetera. Officer Le Fervour from the Fraternal

Order of Police will slap you on the wrists,
convince you to join the Panthers. You will
learn to remember your meals, record

conversations, how to write backwards
in the dark. Monitor all nefarious
activity, the Breakfast for Children Program,

the grits, the jelly. Relax and your body will
float naturally. After you become Minister
of Security, Special Agent M will contact you

intermittently to obtain the locations of weapons
and boxes of cereal. All milk shall be burned
in due time. Give your brother sleeping

pills drowned in water so he won't hear
our fire; after his file closes you'll see plans
of the headquarters*slash*bedrooms we drew

from your eyes. You never even raised
a fist. Take your two hundred bones
for years of uniquely rendered service

and keep treading, remembering to breathe.

Booty Green

From the outside he's a killer
        & we know it.
We've tried hemming Chris inside,

        below the key—
started off playing HORSE
        then quickly switched

to BULLSHIT soon as parents
        headed on indoors—
come dusk, we begin

        telling lies
about length & behind-
        the-back shots,

about how sweet
        our selves are. We've given up
the simon says of Around the World

        ———

for Booty Green, a game
        like 21, only meaner—
blacker, jack.

        The rules: are none.
The rules: no fouls
        called, no traveling,

no out-of-bounds. Just play,
        boy, all elbows & ass
whuppins, fatal angles.

        Amri—his name
a lion—barrels down
        the lane like a shotgun

bride. Rejected.
        Yo mama.
Troy hanging from the rim

———

like a suicide, saving
himself. The shortest,
    I let them fight it out

in the paint, preying
    on rebounds—believe it
or not—learning to toss up

    hooks along the side, their arc
high, sly as a covenant. Mo Fo
    of the Sacred Swish, her

holiness. *And so*
    it came to pass—
but we keep it, head instead

    for the bucket
as if an endzone, gaining air
    like the black balcony

———

of the movie theater, talking
    back to the screens
we each post. The ball

    popcorn to toss.
Brick. *Chump,*
    I thot you knew.

The Easter we've just eaten—
    we angel against
each other till borne

    by air, gaining ground
on God. Between the garage
    & someone's mama's

car—*Watch the paint,*
    nigger—we soar
& psych & sing.

───

Here, to stuff
don't mean your mouth or the Resurrection
   bird now splayed

open indoors, but grabbing the rim
   like a grenade pin. Not
that I'd know. Fingers round

the hoop, an eye
   jabbed soft in its socket—
my glasses fly, a bird

   almost extinct. No apology—
cowboying, we pick up
   & go again, pound the pavement

to pidgin, palming the ball
   the way Chris would grab
smaller boys' foreheads—

───

Crystal ball, tell me all—
his hands reading fortunes
   we pretend we'll make.

Out here we charge, trying
   to father ourselves—
our dads inside, wise,

   where it's still warm.
We laugh at the way
   Chris, like the god he thought

he was, took a new last name—
   Fontaine—trying to pull down
babes on the rebound. Don't

   know how with that
jheri curl juice. But today, fool,
   all our heads are clean

—

as dinner-table talk, as a broke dick
        dog. Our dads asleep
in front of the game

        or divorced, having dinner
with new families—or alone—
        while over dirty dishes

        our mothers laugh.
Here on this angly, angry
        asphalt, no matter what

the songs say, love or faith
        don't make the grade—
one manchild against the rest,

        we dog each other out
so later we can take shots
        from the outside

—

where Chris breaks free,
        prodigal, almost to the lawn—
his jumper murder. Every sunk

        shot sends him to the line,
the rest of us panting
        & bent & catching

breath. If he misses
        it's sudden death
& we're all hoping

        to reach 21. *Last requests?*
he says bouncing
        that ball bald

as a granny, or a baby,
        two things
we're trying to prove

———

    we're not. *No way,*
we holler. Up again
      for the rebound, savior

that never comes—the ball falling
      like a guillotine, or the pumpkin
the executioner tests it on,

      falling like the dark
we barely notice has grown up
      around us—the gruff

voice of a father
      summoning us inside
to dine on humble pie & crow

before it grows cold.

Brown

for my mother

The scrolled brown arms
    of the church pews curve
like a bone—their backs

bend us upright, standing
    as the choir enters
singing, *We've come this far*

by faith—the steps
    & sway of maroon robes,
hands clapping like a heart

in its chest—*leaning*
    on the Lord—
this morning's program

still warm
    from the mimeo machine
quick becomes a fan.

In the vestibule latecomers
    wait just outside
the music—the river

we crossed
    to get here—
wide boulevards now

———

in disrepair.
       We're watched over
    in the antechamber

by Rev.
       Oliver Brown,
    his small, colored picture

nailed slanted
       to the wall—former
    pastor of St. Mark's

who marched
       into that principal's office
    in Topeka to ask

Why can't my daughter
       school here, just
    steps from our house—

but well knew the answer—
       & Little Linda
    became an idea, became more

what we needed & not
       a girl no more—*Free-dom*
    Free-dom—

———

Now meant
        sit-ins & *I shall I shall*
    I shall not be

moved—
        & four little girls bombed
    into tomorrow

in a church basement like ours
        where nursing mothers & children
    not ready to sit still

learned to walk—Sunday school
        sent into pieces
    & our arms.

We are
        swaying more
    now, entering

heaven's rolls—the second row
        behind the widows
    in their feathery hats

& empty nests, heads heavy
        but not hearts
    Amen. The all-white

            ———

stretchy, scratchy dresses
    of the missionaries—
   the hatless holy who pin lace

to their hair—bowing
    down into pocketbooks
   opened for the Lord, then

snapped shut
    like a child's mouth
   mouthing off, which just

one glare from an elder
    could close.
   God's eyes must be

like these—aimed
    at the back row
   where boys pass jokes

& glances, where Great
    Aunts keep watch,
   their hair shiny

as our shoes
    &, as of yesterday,
   just as new—

—

chemical curls & lop-
          sided wigs—humming
     during offering

Oh my Lord
          Oh my Lordy
     What can I do.

The pews curve like ribs
          broken, barely healed,
     & we can feel

ourselves breathe—
          while Mrs. Linda Brown
     Thompson, married now, hymns

piano behind her solo—
          No finer noise
     than this—

We sing
          along, or behind,
     mouth most

every word—following
          her grown, glory voice,
     the black notes

          ⎯⎯⎯

rising like we do—
    like Deacon
    Coleman whom my mother

always called *Mister*—
    who'd help her
    weekends & last

I saw him my mother
    offered him
    a slice of sweet potato

pie as payment—
    or was it apple—
    he'd take no money

barely said
    yes, only
    I could stay

for a piece—
    trim as his grey
    moustache, he ate

with what I can only
    call dignity—
    fork gently placed

———

across his emptied plate.
Afterwards, full,
Mr. Coleman's *That's nice*

meant wonder, meant
the world entire.
Within a year cancer

had eaten him away—
the only hint of it
this bitter taste for a whole

year in his mouth. *The resurrection
and the light.*
For now he's still

standing down front, waiting
at the altar for anyone
to accept the Lord, rise

& he'll meet you halfway
& help you down
the aisle—

legs grown weak—
*As it was in the beginning
Is now*

———

And ever shall be—
    All this tuning
    & tithing. We offer

our voices up
    toward the windows
    whose glass I knew

as colored, not stained—
    our backs
    made upright not by

the pews alone—
    the brown
    wood smooth, scrolled

arms grown
    warm with wear—
    & prayer—

Tell your neighbor
    next to you
    you love them—till

we exit
    into the brightness
    beyond the doors.

FIELD
RECORDINGS

*Dearly Beloved, we are gathered here together
to get through this thing called life.*

—PRINCE

THREE

Night Train

James Brown at B. B. King's on New Year's Eve

The one thing that can solve most
our problems is dancing. And sweat,
cold or not. And burnt ends
of ribs, or reason, of hair
singed & singing. The hot comb's
caress. Days after
he dies, I see James Brown still
scheduled to play B. B. King's
come New Year's Eve—ringing
it in, us, falling to the floor
like the famous glittering midnight
ball drop, countdown, forehead full
of sweat, *please, please,*
please, please, begging
on his knees. The night
King was killed, shot
by the Memphis moan in a town
where B. B. King sang, Saint
James in Boston tells
the crowd: cool it. A riot
onstage, heartache
rehearsed, practiced, don't dare
be late or miss a note
or you'll find yourself fined
fifty bucks. A fortune. Even
the walls sweat. A God-
father's confirmation suit,
his holler, wide-collared, grits
& greens. Encore. Exhausted
after, collapsed, carried
out, away, off—not on a gurney,
no bedsheet over
his bouffant, conk
shining, but, boots on,
in a cape glittering bright
as midnight, or its train.

Fishbone

I found your first
   record yesterday—
it looked like the past

& sounded
   like the future—
that combo platter I love best

of all. The black grooves gave
   way to moans
of horns, yelps,

bass that leapt
   like you did
on the cover—bald,

mohawked, knotted
   & dreaded, bespoke
& be-hatted, daytime shades

& handkerchiefs
   like a bank robber—
plaits & plaids on tweed

like gangster professors.
   One of you grins,
most the rest

in mid-air soar.

[CHECKERBOARD VANS]

The apocalypse sounds
   like this—
black men breaking in

to steal back the thing
   once stole
from them. A drum

trash talking, trombone
   tossed from off
stage into Angelo's hands

less slid than shoved—
   swift notes
swim past—then he throws

the horn back
   like a salmon
into the wings, careless,

rehearsed. After Murphy's Law
   & the Beastie
Boys open the show

even Fishbone's keyboard
   player dervishes,
his body flung

like an epithet
   into the fourth row's
wishbone arms.

[CREEPERS]

Declaring nothing,
    we'd cross customs,
dreads tucked

under our hats—
    once inside
Spain or Paris, London

or some club, we'd let
    loose & dance.
Give me the cheapest

thing they have,
    says Davíd
so I bring him bitters

which even the bartender
    declares undrinkable.
Davíd refuses

to say so, tries choking
    down the pint
like pride. We never ate anyway

sitting down, Davíd always
    looking for a cheaper
bite elsewhere, our stomachs

knotting & our hair. Eyes
    mostly open,
Philippe & I drank & swam

through the dark waters
    of Camdentown, high
on spliff & curry

our new friends cooked.
    We black folks
invented all music

say our Australian-
     Pakistani-British
friends. Everything then

shone in the blacklight—
     our teeth
turnt violet.

We drank at the End
     of the World,
pints three quid

& bitters far less—
     would catch a taxi home
with those suicide

doors, watching the dawn
     leak early above the low,
unopened buildings—

facing backwards
     in the cab black
& shiny as a hearse, staring

at the wherever
     we'd been, we slid
at every turn.

[DOC MARTENS]

Once I saved the bass
    player from Fishbone
from getting his ass

handed to him, but not
    before the fools bloodied
his lip & turnt

his pockets inside out
    like a wish. All because,
Kendall, you refused

to rumble in that late night
    chicken joint
where Philippe & I thought we'd die

as the regulars tried
    picking a fight
with your bright

red coat, dreads
    against your shoulder blades
like epaulets. The club we'd all been

now shut for the night—
    the one Philippe & I had waited
outside of an hour, trying not

to beg. No one's getting in—
    then a posse with locks
longer than us & worse haircuts,

which is to say, cooler,
    part the ropes—
Fishbone!

in London to play a show
    so we sneak in
behind them, for tonight

just another
    of the crew.
Every dread danced.

Starving, after, we enter the shack
    to find you taunted
by locals, loudmouths

who nick your change
    & call you names.
Yankee, one says, shoving you

who refuses, you say,
    to battle another man
who's black. Once his crew

jumps you & runs through
    the street, we reel you in,
Kendall, stop you from chasing them

into the night, insulted
    as much as anything
to be alive—*Back home, South*

Central, you say, *I'd be dead.*
    Your breath itself
a rebuke, passport

a passing memory.
    In the cab we hail
& pay to ride you

back to your hotel, pacifism
    gives way—
wounded not just

by the blows, you fume—
    angry at being
here but no longer

whole. In the lobby,
    we take your manager's
payback & his promise

to leave us passes
    for tomorrow's show.
Was it shame,

honor, or disbelief,
    didn't
let us go?

Months later I caught Fishbone
    in New York at a church
turned into a night club

trying to film the video
    for a song I still
don't know. The one

we'd saved now gone,
    decamped across Europe
believing in something

no longer. Neither
    did you all, it seemed—
the gleam gone, everything

upright, no diving—
    nothing cockamamie
or incomplete. We clap

on cue. Lip sunk, you must
    repeat the song over
& over so the shifting camera

can capture you. Where had all
    the altars gone?
Even my girlfriend an ex.

Even my memory like the mic
    sounds faulty.
Feedback fills the air

& we exit early, back
    to our little boxes
before the song is done—

come morning,
    our ears will still
like church bells toll.

Lead Belly's First Grave

is grey, plain, lowdown.
    You have to crouch
near the ground to get

your picture made
    beside it like Allen Ginsberg
& Robert Plant did, pilgrims

to where the music gave way
    or starts. The stone's
simple dates—birth, death—

shade the close-cropped grass
    & the small pale flowers
someone plucked & offered up

or planted here beneath
    a tree. The stone, silvery,
could be lead instead—

soft & heavy as his voice
    & as deadly, slow.
His new tomb's

tall almost
    as a man—black,
sleek, costly.

Alongside it James Dickey
    grins, elbow resting
on the stone like the shoulder

of a friend. The marker's not
    inelegant, the sepulcher
not quite the sheen

of the suits Lead Belly wore
    soon as he threw off
the chains of the gang

for good, string-ties
    & not the prison stripes
Alan Lomax would have him wear.

Huddie Ledbetter's
    second grave lists
his legend, has this

slab with a guitar engraved
    & a black gate
to keep out the green—

hard to reach, easy
    to read, there's now
no need to kneel.

It

It's rained for days.

He used to hate
    hanging upside
down, now he can't

get enough,
    my son. At the bank
of elevators he bets

which one will arrive first
    & is most times
right. He's nine. Tonight

another neighbor
    & good friend
called him *nigger.* I hear

the boys were all playing
    a game called Lovie—
the point

is to call the It
    names—*bitch,
motherfucker, ass,* they say,

& now *nigger,* who only he
    dare not be.
The good thing

about this rain is that
    his hair curls
even more & looks lush

& untamed. The bad
    thing: this rain,
the wrong elevator

dinging down.

Ode to Big Pun

I'm not a prayer
I just wish a lot

De La Soul Is Dead

A ROLLER SKATING JAM NAMED SATURDAYS

We were black then, not yet
African American, so we danced
every chance we could get.
Thursday & Saturdays we'd chant

*The roof! The roof! The roof
is on fire! We don't need no water*
& folks' perms began to turn.
We had begun to dread

or wear locks anyway, our temples
we'd fade. We said *word*
& *def,* said *dang* & *down* & *fly*—
we gave no goodbyes,

just *Alright then,* or *Bet.*
No one was dead yet.

PEOPLE WHO DIED [JIM CARROLL BAND]

No one was dead yet.
Not that some didn't try.
Often, friends of mine—
These are people who died

died—weekends drank too much
then broke into the pool & swam
though I was barely good at that.
The bottom I never did touch.

Home, almost dried, we'd listen
for the dawn, or to *Mista Dobalina,*
Mista Bob Dobalina—gloryhallastupid—
doused in eyeliner or lycra

& that was just the boys.
Our favorite song was noise.

JUNGLE BOOGIE [24-7 SPYZ]

Our favorite song was noise.
Or Public Enemy turned up
past 10, a hype we'd not believe.
To get hype was the point—

to light out as sexy Star Trek
or as Scooby & his snacks, to chant
Black Music—Black Music—
& drop down as low as we can.

Fight the Power. Fuck
tha police. Break the grip of shame.
*We're 24-7 Spyz—who the fuck
are you.* Tomorrow in flames,

we'll rouse & march—tonight, play
Jungle Boogie, hoping someone will stay.

IF I WAS YOUR GIRLFRIEND

Hoping that someone would stay,
we readied tape decks & dubs
that flipped over to play
all night, like love—

that word we didn't dare speak.
Why else did they invent drink?
except to excuse each mistake,
each deep kiss or steady rut

who, for days after, you'd duck.
Fire alarms were how we knew
who was zooming who. Or whom.
Morning's for sleep; late night we'd talk;

dinner was for getting dressed at last,
anything, so long as it's black.

EVERYBODY [BLACK BOX]

As long as it is black,
the record cut
like a dj track—
those 12-inches we spin

then quit dancing only
to re-arm again. *Everybody,*
Everybody, Everybody,
Everybody, O Everybody—

this was back when
we were almost African
American & black was just
who you were

not what you did. Or who.
And the night was black too.

THE SCENARIO

The two of us, black, met one night
dancing alongside each other to Tribe
at a party in the world's smallest room.
Someone from Carolina brought moon-

shine & over the beat, the clanking heat,
Philippe leaned over his date
to say, Hey man, we should be friends.
What you know yo. And that

was that. Popping the caps off brown
Red Stripe bottles with his teeth
he'd drink out the side of his mouth,
sly. We heads kept ours dreaded, crowned—

a decade later he was gone.
The Scenario, our favorite of 500 songs.

FUNKIN' LESSON

The Scenario. They Want EFX.
Fu-Schnickens. PRT. X-Clan.
The humpty dance
is your chance. The Funky Diabetic

Five-Footer rapping, *I like em brown*
yellow Puerto Rican & Haitian—
& Brazilian & Jamaican
& Maori & half-Nigerian

& Cablinasian & Perusian—
we can get down we can
we can get down. Queen
Latifah's Law. Electric Relaxation.

Buddy buddy. 93 'Til Infinity.
Vainglorious. Passing me by.

WHEN YOU WERE MINE

Nothing passed us by. *Baby,*
you're much too fast. In 1990
we had us an early 80s party—
nostalgic already,

I dug out my best
OPs & two polos, fluorescent,
worn simultaneously—
collar up, pretend preppy.

When Blondie came on—
Rapture, be pure—
things really got going & then
the dancing got shut down

by some square.
What was sleep even for?

HOUSEQUAKE

What was sleep even for?
The year before, a freshman, I threw
a Prince party, re-screwed
the lights red & blue—

the room all purple, people
dancing everywhere—clicked
PLAY on the cassette till
we slow-sweated to Erotic

City, or Do Me Baby. *I'm going down
to Alphabet Street.* Did anyone
sleep alone that night? I Feel
For You. *Shut up already, damn—*

cabbage patch, reverse running man—
get some life wherever you can.

POTHOLES IN MY LAWN

This life. I confess we did look
somewhat alike, Kenny & I—
baby dreads, tortoiseshells, tight fade—
though that night his giant white roommate

drunk on 8 Ball in the pool room
called out *Kenny, Kenny,* even when
I said I'm not him & he began
cursing me out—*Quit pretending*—

that was too much. Dopplegangers,
unblood brothers, we should have done
more with it—dressed as the other
for Halloween, chanced

an evil twin movie. No dice.
Instead we danced, side by side.

THREE IS THE MAGIC NUMBER

Twins to the rhythm, we danced,
as one does—to the remix of Three
Is the Magic Number—at a house party
someone threw just because.

We were black then, about to be
African American, so folks schoolhouse rocked
& smurfed whenever we damn well pleased.
We should have done more, or believed,

mon frère, mine own body double—
given the campus cops the slip
whenever they quizzed or frisked us
for studying while black. Kenny,

I hope you're somewhere
far from here, dancing away trouble.

RING THE ALARM [DUB MIX]

Far from here, dancing away troubles,
Philippe & I nod & bob & start
to skank in the underground club
in London, the dub

so loud across the gigantic room
we feel it in our lungs.
We were never young.
Even then in the bass & boom—

the DJ's fits & starts, the woofer's glottal
guttural gasp, our ganja-throated rasp—
we were old, though not enough
to know. That time he sat silent for hours

in the corner, high on soul flower? *You're
messing up my plan,* all he could say, after.

SOUL FLOWER [BRAND NEW HEAVIES]

Afterwards, what can I say, unplanned,
a decade later, he was dead. Forget friends;
brothers. Forget it all except how
the sun is coming up now

between the buildings—
is it night, or morning—
dawn coming on, we hated
leaving any party early. I hate

having to write what
can never capture how thin
everything was then—
the beer, or warm cider,

or us—yet strong enough, son,
to get the job done.

I NEED LOVE

I get the job done, baby,
I work. Nobody
can rap quite like
I can. I'll take

you there. Ain't no
half steppin. Ain't no-
body. Ain't too proud
to beg. Ain't no

mountain high enough.
It's only mountains.
And the sea. See
what you done done?

I'm so tired of being alone.
I wonder if I take you home.

FAST CAR [TRACY CHAPMAN]

Taking her home those weeks
of winter break, dorm snowed in, no one
around but us, I'd ask
her, late, to sing to me alone.

Here in Subcity, life is hard—
naked behind her guitar
she'd do her best Tracy Chapman,
twin bed her smallest stage. *Please give*

the President my honest regards. We'd fall
asleep in her room—bedframe
narrow as a grave—but not quite
in love. Our huddled nights

wouldn't survive the thaw,
snow gone too soon, & far.

U GOT THE LOOK

Gone too soon, there was that season
when all the ladies' bras
bloomed suddenly fancy because
by midnight we knew everyone

would be shirtless, one
giant groove, swaying along
to Gett Off, or Funky Drummer
(Parts 1 & 2), or Sexy M.F.—

all innocent somehow, beauty
on the installment plan.
At least till the horns swoop in.
This ain't about the body

it's about the mind.
Yours, or mine?

WHEN DOVES CRY

Yours or mine? From this
great a distance
I cannot tell which Prince
records are my father's

& which I bought alone. Pop hated Prince
at first, said he couldn't sing, nor dance.
(Then again, neither could he.) Once
Purple Rain dropped, I flew home from France

& he asked, Have you heard this?
The spool of the car's tape deck
& it's the chorus: *This is
what it sounds like*. Sneaky devil,

maybe I'm just like my father,
my mother silent in the car.

I WOULD DIE 4 U

My mother silent all the way
home, not knowing what to say
or sing. Me, mugged in Paris two days
before & then, Easter Sunday,

a knife pulled on us
high schoolers from Kansas
on the metro to Notre Dame, always
mispronounced. How I prayed

the entire ride, saw the madman's
pockets blooming blades. *Take Me
With U*. After, at madrigals the psalms
barely came. My folks' marriage

even my father's newfound love
of Prince couldn't save.

LITTLE WING

Save us. So late & still
our sophomore roommate
has decided to pull
out his guitar, plug in & play

Little Wing, just the first bars,
over & over, *take anything
you want from me,* till we only
want him to finish, to get, for once,

to the end. Years later,
he'll kill himself—I still don't
know how, much less fathom
why. Carey Monserrate,

last name a mountain,
play for us again.

ALL THAT I GOT IS YOU [RADIO EDIT]

Play it again: soon all will be gone, the places
I've known; Elsie's, The Tasty, Tommy's Lunch
replaced by lobster & *prix fixe* brunch.
The cobbler one day disappears like the very

word *cobbler*. My dry cleanser now does shoe repair.
One Potato Two Potato. That druggist I never
went to. Slowly every bookstore shut down
or moved—Star, McIntyre & Moore—

put out like lights. *After 180 Years We're Closing
Our Doors.* Even the Wursthaus—its food
earning its name—I miss avoiding, proving
yourself no more a tourist. If lucky we leave

not just a place but a name. Soon, all gone:
Tommy's, The Tasty, Elsie's, me.

BUNGLE IN THE JUNGLE

Me, Thomas, & everyone
crammed into his room bright
as a club at closing for the Bungle
in the Jungle, that party whose goal

was to get as naked as possible
without going the whole way. I came,
not literally, in silkish green paisley
boxers, little else. Shoes, maybe.

Once we blew the bass
blasting Respect or Groove
Is in the Heart, Thomas shouts
To the pool! & the parade

heads thataway, a hundred Adams
& Eves splashing, making waves.

FISHERMAN'S BLUES [THE WATERBOYS]

Making waves, I was just plugging in
a boombox when the counselor
came & screamed *Kevin—*
get these people out of here. Later

the pool sprung an unlikely leak,
got closed for good & ill & us.
Later still I'd climb down with Seamus—
no shallows—to watch a different play

with my roommate far more nude
confessing in Act Two, a-swim in a giant suit,
than the first when he was mad Sweeney
cursed naked & muddy in a tree.

Nice allegory, offered Heaney. Far was fate
it felt; how could we know how late?

THE LAST DAY OF OUR ACQUAINTANCE

How late it would get.
Every party
was an after-party.
Some nights we'd even let

ourselves forget that dawn
would soon come. *I do not want
what I haven't got.* Mostly it did.
Sometimes the morn was met

less alone, her beauty & scent,
her buzzed head numbing your arm.
Once you start, how can you quit
all this remembering? We make

love like memories, if lucky
& not too late.

THE CHOICE IS YOURS

Too late. The silence, ours,
now sounds like the second
when the music stops—
not for good, but for a breath

or two, *engine engine*
number nine on the New York
transit line, if my train
jumps off the track—

& now we're back up.
O how high we jump.
Reaching for the sky
hurricane-purple & a night

mostly black, dark blue, red.
Nobody, nobody, was dead. Yet—

Ode to Ol Dirty Bastard

F you. Motor
mouth, clown
of class warfare,

welfare millionaire—
how dare you disappear
when we need your

shimmy shimmy ya
here. Osirus
of this shiznit, your body's

now scattered
on wax. No monument,
no fortune left—

just what you made
& spent, I hope, on skunk
weed & worse. *Good*

morning heartache.
Your carelessness
reminds us how

quick we are
to judge, how
serious things

done become. Dirty
as the south, sweet
as neon cherry pie

filling from a can.
I hear folks still call
your number in Brooklyn

all hours
& ask the sleepy, still
listed Russell Jones

(no relation)
come out & play.
Baby, I got

your money.
Big Baby Jesus, Dirt
McGirt, alias-addict—

of course you can't
be reached—
you're too busy, Rusty,

wigging out, dancing
in a humpsuit & jheri curl
toupee, your tiny,

tacky dreads
hidden, your grill
of gold melted

down to pay off
St. Pete, or Beezlebub,
to buy just one more

dose of freedom.

FOUR

The Crescent Limited

B. B. King Plays Oxford, Mississippi

A poetry where Saturday night
    meets Sunday morning,
a midnight music,

a crossroads sound—
    coming home from the juke
& heading right to church

for sunrise service
    & maybe catch a bit
of that communion wine.

Butterbeans.
    You know I'm from Mississippi
I do carry a knife.

Everybody wants to go to heaven
    but nobody wants to die
to get there.

Time to go
    a little further
up the alley—

I got a good mind
    to give up living
& go shopping instead

to pick out a tombstone
    & be
pronounced dead.

Bass

Where was the music from?
    The bass that woke my son
sleeping in his room, mom

out of town,
    so alone
I'd sung him home.

He was just about down
    when the beat began
faraway, filling our noses

& chests like morning
    coffee, which I don't take any
kind of way—though black

is what you can say
    when they ask
& they will. Brown boy,

head back & dream.

An hour later his busy brain
    stirs him again,
descending the steep

stairs to ask to sleep
    beside me on the couch,
cat-curled, quieted

at last. I rise
    & search the windows to see
if I might spot the sound—

still going, louder now,
    its thin thunder
reaching me, everywhere,

even here.

Triptych for Trayvon Martin

NOT GUILTY [A FRIEZE FOR SANDRA BLAND]

Because the night has no
   number, because
the thunder doesn't

   mean rain
Because maybe
   Because we must

say your names
   & the list grows
longer & more

   endless
I am writing this:
   you are no gun

nor holster, no
   finger aimed, thumb
a hammer cocked

   back, all the way—
I refuse
   to bury you, to inter

your name in earth
   or to burn you back
to bone, to what

   we all know, the soft
song of your skull
   as an infant, the place

God or your mother
   or same thing
left untouched

   by hands—
that halo grown whole
   till they said you weren't—

said that Death
    could be your breath—
could be a body

    or less—& you
grew more black
    & blue.

I refuse
    to watch. I refuse.
Not guilty. Not

    guilty. I know you
will stay & rise
    like the sea—

the tide
    all salt & shifting.
Don't ever leave.

LIMBO [A FRESCO FOR TAMIR RICE]

Skeleton-still,
    we stood. Those
before us who

Believed, arrayed
    like statues, trophies
of the child killed

We couldn't bear
    to dust
or box away.

The dark arch
    to the lost teen's
bedroom, jersey

Now empty, baseball team
    down a man—
out with an injury.

Wild pitch. Passed ball.
    Technical knockout.
Technical foul.

Flagrant two. The flagration
    of the car turned over
he lay dead beside

A good while.
    Dark dye
seeping into the street.

No pop flies. No catch—
    player to be
named later—

No sheet we'll provide—
    Just the blue-tail fly
doornailed, hungry,

Fit to die.

NIGHTSTICK [A MURAL FOR MICHAEL BROWN]

There are gods
    of fertility,
corn, childbirth,

& police
    brutality—this last
is offered praise

& sacrifice
    near weekly
& still cannot

be sated—many-limbed,
    thin-skinned,
its colors are blue

& black, a cross-
    hatch of bruise
& bulletholes

punched out
    like my son's
three-hole notebooks—

pages torn
    like lungs, excised
or autopsied, splayed

open on a cold table
    or left in the street
for hours to stew.

A finger
    is a gun—
a wallet

is a gun, skin
    a shiny pistol,
a demon, a barrel

already ready—
    hands up
don't shoot—

arms
    not to bear
but bare. Don't

dare take
    a left
into the wrong

skin. Death
    is not dark
but a red siren

who will not blow
    breath into your open
mouth, arrested

like a heart. Because
    I can see
I believe in you, god

of police brutality—
    of corn liquor
& late fertility, of birth

pain & blood
    like the sun setting,
dispersing its giant

crowd of light.

A Brown Atlanta Boy Watches Basketball on West 4th. Meanwhile, Neo-Nazis March on Charlottesville, Virginia.

Here the pain
    mostly goes away.
A stinger someone tries

walking off, his face a mask.
    He's giving you
the ball Jay,

he's giving you the ball—
    Gary with the attack—
Thaddeus is having

the game of his life,
    the MC says. Old men
watch in their grey mustaches

mouthing salt peanuts—
    or toothpicks,
or day-old gum—

chewing the fat.
    You see that?
He needs to just put

that back up.
    The uniforms black
& blue as a bruise.

Must ignore the need
    cuz we the news—
here every call

is wrong, all
    fouls technical—
even here black

means guest, not home.
    Forget about the refs,
they already told us

shut up. It's us
    against them
Let's go.

Howlin' Wolf

In Parchman   Prison
in stripes   standing
guitar gripped   like a neck
strangled   strummed
high strung   & hard.
Mostly   you moan
see how   heavy
your hands   hang with-
out women   or words
we cannot
quite know.   How is this
not hell   being made
to make music   here where
music only   makes time
go slow   cloudy
like blue
Depression glass?   Under
the hard sun   of your smile
we see   stripes like those
that once   lined the slave's
unbent back
blood   & gunk
spit   it out
a song   low down
gutbucket
built   for comfort
not built   for speed.
Gimme   the brack
of the body   the blue
the bile   all
you sing   or howl.
If a wolf   then lone
then orphan   then *hangry*
enough to enter   into town
to take food   from the mouths
of low houses   a hen
a stray   it is never
enough.   You don't need
tell me   why
we here   you know

better   black
as an exclamation   point
the men   all around
you   in stripes
how long   their sentences
their dark   faces ellipses
everywhere accidental.
The white   man
in front   proud
or is it   prideful
he wears   no number
& now   exiled under
the earth   no one
recalls   his name.
Yours   a dark wick
waiting   we burn
wanting you   to step
into song
to again   howl
till you sweat   through
your shirt   & two
white   handkerchiefs
a revival
preacher   waving
praise   no flag
of surrender—
the guitar   a blunt
instrument   your hair
your shoes   even your
voice   shines.

Repast

an oratorio in honor of Mister Booker Wright

of Greenwood, Mississippi

BARKEEP ACTIVIST WAITER

[HOSPITALITY BLUES]

Welcome. Have a seat—
the audience sits.
I insist. I'm your host.
Your money is no
good here, no good
here no good
no good
no good.
Your money is no good.
Here. Your money
is no god here no—Glad
to see you all. We don't
have a written menu
I'll be glad to tell you
what we're going to serve
tonight tonight tonight

Uptempo:
We have fresh shrimp
cocktails Lusco shrimp
fresh oysters on the half shell
baked oysters oysters
Rockefeller oysters almondine
stewed oysters fried oysters
Spanish mackerel broil whetstone
sirloin steak club steak T-bone
steak porterhouse steak ribeye
steak Lusco special steak mushrooms
flavor of garlic Italian spaghetti
& meatballs softshell crab
French fried onions golden
brown donut style
Best food in the world
the world the world
the world is served at Lusco's
He nods & rocks

Tell my people what you got.

[THE HEAD WAITER'S LAMENT]

The hardest thing is knowing
when you're free. Easy

to see when you're not—
when the wind don't

make a dent in how the fig
falls from the tree, or your

mouth never fed enough—
or your child-

ren, how much
to tell them? *The meaner*

the man be, the more
you smile.

When do you talk
about it, the men—

never one—who come
for you, burning

& cutting & crossing—
even a pistol

can be made a whip—
just for you saying

what's true. Not
what you're taught.

That's a good nigger.
That's my

nigger. Brush your
taut dark hair.

[RESERVATIONS]

Some call me Booker,
some call me John, some

call me Jim, some call me—
This is my place

I say, meaning where
I work but more

the green bar I tend
& keep, the mouths I feed

not only my child-
ren, who I want better for

than me—the slenderest
tall trees. The willows

who weep. What should
my place be? It is loudest

here after the black descends,
gathers in the Mississippi

leaves, first green then
dark like me—my first

name's Mack but nobody
calls me that. I'm named

for a man who made
his name at Tuskegee

which ain't that
far from here

I hear.

[BOOKER'S PLACE]

It's the haze that hurts.
Sometimes far worse
than when the sun

spits its rays
all over your face—
them days you brown

& redden, the work
can be like
to kill you—

so a man need
a place to go inside
his head & walk around

& rest. There's a juke
joint of the soul, somewhere
you can have yourself

something cold, or brown
burning water—we used
to get ice in fresh, cut

from giant blocks,
sawdust, clean glasses
& good good food. I kept

the bar sparkling, shiny
as the teeth of the couples
on calendars behind me

staring into each other's eyes.
Budweiser in cans, Nehi,
Drink Coca-Cola

Bottled up. This was my place—
a green room, a somewhere
you could twist, maybe spin

a partner on the dance floor
or just set a spell
& tap your foot, mine,

taking it all in.
We never let anyone
carry on too long

& made sure they carried
themselves home safe
beside the tracks

that also kept
their crosses, clanging—
that train red,

an eye,
then blue, bearing
down on you.

[WAITING]

So this is what I said:

Now that's what my customers—
I say my customers—

be expecting of me. Booker,
Tell my people what you got.

Some people nice,
some people not.

What's wrong with you
why you not smiling?

Go over & get me
so & so and so & so.

And I keep that smile.
Always learn to smile

Although you're crying
on the inside.

Sometime he'll tip you
Sometime he'll say,

I'm not going to tip
that nigger, he don't look

for no tip. Yessir,
thank you.

What'd you say?
Yes sir, boss,

I'm your nigger.
But remember

you got to keep that smile.
Night after night

I lay down & I dream
about what I had

to go through with.
That's what I'm struggling for.

I'm trying to make
a living.

For this they whipped
me good, but not dead.

[DEATH'S DICTIONARY]

A shack made of ribs.
A house made of out.

A car made of rust.
A smile made of doubt.

A house made of fire.
A magician's gesture.

Of cards. Of the Lord.
As preacher, pats his brow.

A joint made of juke.
A twist. A night away.

A wood made of green.
Of blood.

The kerchief now a bandage.
A place in the sun.

A house made of railroad.
A shack of shotgun.

[A GLOSSARY OF UPPITY]

For *please,* please read
forget you.

For *sun,*
read none.

For *love,* read
money.

For *money,* read.

For *smile,* read
Bless Your Heart.

For *uppity*
read siddity.

For *siddity*
read dicty.

For *dicty,* hincty.

For pleasure.
For unknowing.

For *forgetting*
read mystery.

For *smile*
read speak.

For *hush*
read shush

read shut up
read don't

you dare.
For *dare,* read sure.

For *speak up*
read speak out.

For the *future*
say now.

For my children.
For *ever*.

Thy trumpet
tongue.

Thy work
never done.

For *Thee*—
read We.

[PINING, *A Definition*]

Look like last night
the light hardly wanted

to leave—it hung
round in the pines

for what seemed hours
after the sun said

its goodbyes. Sometimes
can get hard

to just go, you know—
we stand around talking

not noticing the dark
rising up around

our feet.
Stand up & maybe

stretch & see
ourselves home. We

be a gas station dog
waiting for something

to fall, so we
can eat awhile

& sleep. When morning
decides to wake

maybe just this once
it'll be late

& we can join the table
already set, like fate—

welcomed by the knives—
& just from the scent

of something someone we love
cooked for us

feel fed.

Those who are able, please rise—

[SUNDAYING]

And everyone working
the drive-thru is beautiful

smiling just
like the commercial

Thanks, I will
have a good day

& a double
cheeseburger too

And without complaint
the birds wake

you early
sun against the skin

Somewhere smell
of a grill

Cut grass & gasoline

And the church lady
her hat a bouquet

saying Hello

Hello
The sun a giant melon

And we're not getting
any younger

but today no older neither

And why not
live forever

Why not wait
till tomorrow

to pay the phone
the gas electric

Why not pray
for a tie

instead of a win
for the game to go

long, on & on,
a million innings

Whistle

And then he can whistle

this son, moon
   of mine
circling, the name

we gave to the far side
   of the satellite,
this thunder

in the near distance
   heralding summer,
grown thirsty,

plummeting down
   suddenly, drenching
the dog & drought-fed

lawn. Nothing
   for once is wrong—
cicadas quieted,

the rain's metal smell,
   a train on time
arriving

& that sound now his—
   as if a kiss
might make music.

Money Road

for John T. Edge

On the way to Money,
   Mississippi, we see little
ghosts of snow, falling faint

   as words while we try to find
Robert Johnson's muddy
   maybe grave. Beside Little Zion,

along the highwayside, this stone
   keeps its offerings—Bud & Louisiana
Hot Sauce—the ground giving

   way beneath our feet.
The blues always dance
   cheek to cheek with a church—

Booker's Place back
   in Greenwood still standing,
its long green bar

   beautiful, Friendship Church just
a holler away. Shotgun,
   shotgun, shotgun—

———

rows of colored
    houses, as if the same can
of bright stain might cover the sins

    of rotting wood, now
mostly tarpaper & graffiti
    holding McLaurin Street together—

RIP Boochie—the undead walk
    these streets seeking something
we take pictures of

    & soon flee. The hood
of a car yawns open
    in awe, men's heads

peer in its lion's mouth
    seeking their share. FOR SALE:
Squash & *Snap Beans*. The midden

    of oyster shells behind Lusco's—
the tiny O of a bullethole
    in Booker's plate glass window.

———

Even the Salvation
    Army Thrift Store
closed, bars over

    every door.
We're on our way again,
    away, along the Money

Road, past grand houses
    & porte cocheres set back
from the lane, crossing the bridge

    to find markers of what's
no more there—even the underpass
    bears a name. It's all

too grave—the fake
    sharecropper homes
of Tallahatchie Flats rented out

    along the road, staged bottle trees
chasing away nothing, the new outhouse
    whose crescent door foreign tourists

    ———

pay extra for. Cotton planted
   in strict rows
for show. A quiet

   snowglobe of pain
I want to shake.
    While the flakes fall

like ash we race
   the train to reach the place
Emmett Till last

   whistled or smiled
or did nothing.
   Money more

a crossroads
   than the crossroads be—
its gnarled tree—the Bryant Store

   facing the tracks, now turnt
the color of earth, tumbling down
   slow as the snow, white

———

& insistent as the woman
　　who sent word
of that uppity boy, her men

　　who yanked you out
your uncle's home
　　into the yard, into oblivion—

into this store abutting
　　the MONEY GIN CO.
whose sign, worn away,

　　now reads UN
Or SIN, I swear—
　　whose giant gin fans,

like those lashed & anchored
　　to your beaten body,
still turn. Shot, dumped,

　　dredged, your face not even
a mask—a marred,
　　unspared, sightless stump—

　　　　———

all your mother insists
　　we must see to know
What they did

　　to my baby. The true
Tallahatchie twisting south,
　　the Delta

Death's second cousin
　　once removed. You down
for only the summer, to leave

　　the stifling city where later
you will be waked,
　　displayed, defiant,

a dark glass.
　　There are things
that cannot be seen

　　but must be. Buried
barely, this place
　　no one can keep—

———

Yet how to kill
   a ghost? The fog
of our outdoor talk—

   we breathe,
we grieve, we drink
   our tidy drinks. I think

now winter will out—
   the snow bless
& kiss

   this cursed earth.
Or is it cussed? I don't
   yet know. Let the cold keep

still your bones.

Hive

The honey bees' exile
    is almost complete.
You can carry

them from hive
    to hive, the child thought
& that is what

he tried, walking
    with them thronging
between his pressed palms.

Let him be right.
    Let the gods look away
as always. Let this boy

who carries the entire
    actual, whirring
world in his calm

unwashed hands,
    barely walking, bear
us all there

buzzing, unstung.

NOTES & ACKNOWLEDGMENTS

Several poems first appeared in literary magazines and publications; thank you to their editors:

Jai-Alai: Ode to Ol Dirty Bastard

New York Review of Books: Ode to the Harlem Globetrotters

The New Yorker: Money Road; the sonnets "When You Were Mine" and "Housequake" (as "Little Red Corvette"). Special thanks to Paul Muldoon.

Oxford American: Pining, A Definition

QuickMuse: James Brown at B. B. King's

VQR: Repast (minus "Pining")

Zoland Books: Mercy Rule

"Thataway" was commissioned by the Museum of Modern Art to accompany artist Jacob Lawrence's *Migration Series* exhibition and catalog. "Limbo" in the "Triptych for Trayvon Martin" first appeared in MoMa's limited-edition volume of Robert Rauschenberg's *Thirty-four Drawings for Dante's* Inferno, also commissioned. Thanks to Leah Dickerman.

"Open Letter to Hank Aaron" first appeared as part of the exhibition on Hank Aaron at Emory University's Woodruff Library, from spring to fall 2014.

Both "James Brown at B. B. King's" and "Ode to Ol Dirty Bastard" appear in the *Southern Poetry Anthology: Georgia* volume.

"Howlin' Wolf" appears in the anthology *Tales of Two Americas,* edited by John Freeman.

The first line and a half of "James Brown . . ." is a quote from the artist.

"Repast": The *repast* refers to the traditional African American meal following a funeral. Whether formal or for family members only, held at a house of worship or the home of the deceased, catered by a favorite local spot or a community potluck, the repast is a ritual connected to other foodways, as well as to traditions both African and American, Christian and more broadly religious. Where the wake before the funeral is primarily about the dead, the repast is also about the living, who share food and memories. The very word has come to suggest a reflection, not on the past but on the future, a final sup-per after the burial that leaves the circle unbroken.

Repast celebrates the life and bravery of Booker Wright, owner of Booker's Place and waiter at Lusco's in Greenwood, Mississippi, a town quite near to where white racists killed Emmett Till in 1955 and others murdered civil rights workers Goodman, Schwerner, and Cheney in 1963. In 1966, for the NBC documentary *Mississippi: A Self-Portrait,* Wright knowingly spoke out about the double standards and racism of Greenwood's white patrons, many of whom were also featured in the show (and were White Citizens' Council members). After the film aired, Wright was beaten up and sent to a hospital—by a local police officer, no less—and his own establishment firebombed. Both the man and the bar survived. Years later Wright was shot and killed by a bar patron. As described in the recent documentary *Booker's Place,* Wright's descendants and others in the community have suggested that the shooting had a political motivation.

In his own words from the 1966 documentary and through the imagination, Wright speaks of life and foodways in the American South and what it means to wait. Over the course of the piece, his waiter's serving napkin goes from bar towel to preacher's handkerchief, as Wright literally transforms from a waiter to a barkeep to an activist—which may prove the same thing.

The oratorio was commissioned by the Southern Foodways Alliance and debuted at its annual symposium in October 2014, and was reprised at Carnegie Hall on 4 April 2016. Thanks to John T. Edge, Bruce Levingston (pianist and musical director), composer Nolan Gasser, and baritone Justin Hopkins.

"Money Road": "Money Road" traces my driving the Delta with friend and Southern Foodways Alliance leader John T. Edge—we started out visiting Booker's Place in Greenwood, Mississippi, for *Repast,* the oratorio the SFA had commissioned from me on Booker Wright. Turns out Greenwood is where the term Black Power was popularized at a rally by Stokely Carmichael in 1966, just a few blocks from Booker's. Nearly fifty years later one could still see why. Driving to Money that day, it was bitter cold, snow accompanying what became the pilgrimage recorded in the poem. The site of Till's lynching feels both holy and haunted.

In 2017 the news revealed—at least to those who had bought the story—that the white woman at the center of the case, who had claimed Till whistled at her or called her *baby,* confessed that Till had in fact not done a thing. I am heartened that the poem had already said he 'whistled or smiled / or did nothing,' though I still wonder why had even well-meaning southern and American accounts decried the lynching but somehow believed the lynchers? Till's murderers—who lied in court, got acquitted in no time by an all-white jury, then promptly sold their story without fear of reprisal—should not be believed. In some small way perhaps it's because we cannot believe the whole of the truth—that evil does discriminate—much like, in more recent cases from Trayvon Martin to Michael Brown, some cling to some sense of black culpability in their own killings. The poem calls out to us to remember but also to revisit and revise what we think of the past—not in the ways of bluesman Robert Johnson's unlikely gravesite along the Money Road, or the fake plantation there that proves almost as haunting—but in the reality of the now-crumbling storefront where Till was brought and then killed in the night for no earthly, or only earthly, reasons.

My gratitude to Melanie Dunea for the photographs in these pages. With support from the *Virginia Quarterly Review,* she traveled with me to the Mississippi Delta in January 2015 to capture the spirit of that place with a poetry that enhances my own.

A NOTE ABOUT THE AUTHOR

Kevin Young is the director of the Schomburg Center for Research in Black Culture and poetry editor for *The New Yorker*. He is the author of thirteen books of poetry and prose, including *Blue Laws: Selected & Uncollected Poems 1995–2015,* long-listed for the National Book Award; and *Book of Hours,* a finalist for the Kingsley Tufts Poetry Award and winner of the Lenore Marshall Prize from the Academy of American Poets. Young's most recent nonfiction book, *Bunk: The Rise of Hoaxes, Humbug, Plagiarists, Phonies, Post-Facts, and Fake News,* was a *New York Times* Notable Book and a finalist for the National Book Critics Circle Award. His collection *Jelly Roll: A Blues* was a finalist for both the National Book Award and the Los Angeles Times Book Prize for Poetry. His first nonfiction book, *The Grey Album: On the Blackness of Blackness,* won the Graywolf Press Nonfiction Prize and the PEN Open Book Award. A University Distinguished Professor at Emory, Young is the editor of eight other collections and was inducted into the American Academy of Arts and Sciences in 2016.

A NOTE ON THE TYPE

The text of this book was composed in Apollo, the first type-
face ever originated specifically for film composition. Designed
by Adrian Frutiger and issued by the Monotype Corporation of
London in 1964, Apollo is not only a versatile typeface suitable
for many uses but also pleasant to read in all of its sizes.

Composed by North Market Street Graphics,
Lancaster, Pennsylvania

Printed and bound by Berryville Graphics,
Berryville, Virginia

Endpapers by Mack Young

Designed by Maggie Hinders